THE UNAUTHORIZED BIOGRAPHY

SCOOP!

ISSUE #8

Zendaya

by Jennifer Poux

D1523979

Grosset & Dunlap

GROSSET & DUNLAP
An Imprint of Penguin Random House LLC, New York

Illustrations by Becky James

Photo credits: cover: Jon Kopaloff/Stringer/FilmMagic/Getty Images

Copyright © 2020 by Penguin Random House LLC. All rights reserved.
Published by Grosset & Dunlap, an imprint of Penguin Random House LLC, New York.
GROSSET & DUNLAP is a registered trademark of Penguin Random House LLC.
Printed in the USA.

Visit us online at www.penguinrandomhouse.com.

ISBN 9780593222560   10 9 8 7 6 5 4 3 2 1

TABLE OF CONTENTS

• •

CHAPTER 1

WHAT'S IN A NAME?

*L*et's get something straight: It's pronounced Zen-DAY-uh. Not Zen-DIE-uh.

And don't bother with a last name. She has one—it's Coleman. But she doesn't use it, professionally at least. Why just the one name, you ask?

"I just thought it was cool, like Cher or Prince," Zendaya told *Allure*.

"Cool" could be Zendaya's middle name—it's a word people often use to describe her. But her parents aren't that cruel. She was born Zendaya Maree Stoermer Coleman. Her name is a road map to her complex heritage, which *is* really cool. Zendaya's father was born Samuel David Coleman but took an African name, Kazembe Ajamu, reflecting his ancestry. Zendaya's mom, Claire

Marie Stoermer, is of German, Scottish, and other European heritage.

"I get like a mixture of all the worlds," she told *Us Weekly*. She has an African first name. And her middle name is French—like's her mom's middle name—but with an African spelling. "I'm proud of the fact that I know where I'm from."

The name Zendaya comes from the Shona word *tendai*, which means to give thanks or be grateful, and her dad's love of the letter *Z*. (Shona is a Bantu language of the Shona people of Zimbabwe.)

Zendaya is gaining household-name status as the actor makes her mark in television and film. But she wasn't always famous. Celebrities start out like the rest of us—ordinary, unknown babies. In Zendaya's case, maybe her parents had a premonition that she would be famous someday and might need a slammin' name.

But she had a pretty unremarkable childhood— at least in the early years. Zendaya was born on September 1, 1996, in Oakland, California. (She says

Here's the **SCOOP!** Zendaya says her grandparents had her colors read when she was still a toddler. Her aura is purple, which means creative. The guy who did the reading told them Zendaya was going to amaze them their whole lives. That prediction came true!

she lived in a "not-so-amazing" neighborhood.) She has five half-brothers and -sisters, but she's the only child of Claire and Kazembe. She was born an aunt: An older sibling already had kids when she came into the world. So she has an older niece and nephew. Awkward! And some younger ones, too.

Back when she was just a regular Oakland kid with a first and last name, Zendaya's parents were teachers and her mom was also the house manager at a local theater, the California Shakespeare Theater in Orinda. Zendaya spent loads of time there. And that's where a little girl got the big idea that she might want to be an actor.

The catch? She was a truly shy kid. Her fans won't be surprised by that info. Zendaya is pretty open about her personality and her proclivity to spend coveted free time at home watching Harry Potter movies and crime documentaries.

Her shyness could be somewhat debilitating when she was a kid. "I wouldn't try anything," Zendaya admits. "I always had this fear of failing and not doing so well."

Here's a double SCOOP! Zendaya was so shy as a kid that her parents had her repeat kindergarten!

Tbh, it's not that unusual for actors and singers to be shy kids. Sometimes people who get nervous around other people or are introverted by nature feel more comfortable onstage, performing. Zendaya calls herself introverted to this day. The introverted-actor thing makes sense if you think about it. There's a separation between you and the audience. And you're playing the part of a character—the stage lets you be someone else. There's relief in that if you sometimes find it difficult to be yourself.

Whatever she was experiencing offstage, Zendaya liked to be on it. Her first role was in a production of *James and the Giant Peach*. She was bummed when they cast her as a speechless silkworm. But then, in true Zendaya fashion, she committed—giving her tiny part everything she had. "I was the best silkworm ever," she says in MTV's "The Story of Zendaya." And the cutest!

Like so many actors and singers, Zendaya got started early. There were plays, and theater workshops, and modeling for stores like Macy's. And then came the Disney audition that changed everything. (More on that later!) But unlike a lot of child actors, Zendaya has managed (so far) to maintain a scandal-free life. On her show in 2016, Ellen asked Zendaya how she's avoided that cliché.

"I gotta give it up to my parents. I'm really lucky to have the parents that I have and they just have always instilled in me those core values that I think I have to carry with me through everything."

The more you get to know her, the more you get the impression she's a genuinely nice person with a sense of humility, a woman with her feet firmly planted in the ground and a good head on her shoulders, speaking of clichés.

THE SCOOP! DEETS:

BORN: September. 1, 1996
BIRTHPLACE: Oakland, CA
BIRTH NAME: Zendaya Maree Stoermer Coleman
SIGN: Virgo
PARENTS: Claire Marie Stoermer and Kazembe Ajamu (born Samuel David Coleman)
SIBLINGS: Five older half siblings on dad's side
DOG: Noon, a miniature schnauzer
CULINARY PREFERENCE: Vegetarian
HEIGHT: 5'10"
INSTAGRAM FOLLOWERS: 64 million
STYLIST: Law Roach

Bottom line: She wasn't a spoiled kid, and she hasn't turned into a spoiled adult. When asked by *Vogue*'s "73 Questions" how she would describe her childhood, Zendaya simply said, "Real." Kudos to Claire and Kazembe for that, and kudos to Zendaya for keeping it real.

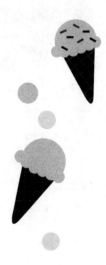

SCOOP! QUIZ

MATCH THESE ONE-NAME CELEBRITIES WITH THEIR SURNAMES

1. Drake	1. Jones
2. Kesha	2. Fenty
3. Oprah	3. Ciccone
4. Adele	4. Ripoll
5. Pink	5. Raymond
6. Usher	6. Sebert
7. Madonna	7. Graham
8. Rihanna	8. Adkins
9. Nas	9. Nelson
10. Lorde	10. Winfrey
11. Prince	11. Moore
12. Shakira	12. Yelich-O'Connor

★ Check your answers on page 93!

THE QUOTABLE SHAKESPEARE

So much of Zendaya's early childhood theater experiences revolved around seeing and performing in Shakespeare's plays in the theater where her mom worked. You might know some of Shakespeare's work, but did you know that many of the expressions we use every day are credited to the sixteenth-century writer? Here are just a few.

★ Break the ice (*The Taming of the Shrew*)
★ Fainthearted (*Henry VI Part I*)
★ For goodness' sake (*Henry VIII*)
★ Good riddance (*Troilus and Cressida*)
★ Jealousy is the green-eyed monster (*Othello*)
★ Heart of gold (*Henry V*)
★ In my mind's eye (*Hamlet*)
★ Laughingstock (*The Merry Wives of Windsor*)

- ★ Love is blind (*The Merchant of Venice*)
- ★ Wear my heart upon my sleeve (*Othello*)
- ★ Wild-goose chase (*Romeo and Juliet*)

Zendaya says her favorite line from Shakespeare is: "If music be the food of love, play on." (*Twelfth Night*)

CHAPTER 2

ZENDAYA SHAKES IT UP AND GOES UNDERCOVER

*T*ween Zendaya hadn't done much professional work when she walked into that Disney audition ready to roll. The very tall twelve-year-old had been a backup dancer in a Sears commercial starring Selena Gomez, and had appeared in an *iCarly* toy ad. Plus she did some modeling and other dancing. But that was about it. (She was signed with Miley Cyrus's agent, so there's also that.)

"I just popped up out of nowhere," she told *Allure*. "I came. I knew what I wanted. I think they saw that." Um . . . let's just say she came and she conquered.

Originally, Zendaya auditioned for the role of

CeCe in *Shake It Up*, performing Michael Jackson's "Leave Me Alone." But the producers asked her to read for the character Rocky Blue, and *bam!* She nailed it, landing the role and leaving two hundred Rocky hopefuls in the dust.

"I had a connection with her character. And when I went with Bella [Thorne] it was like instant chemistry. So I guess it worked out for the best," she told *J-14*.

There was a downside to it all: Zendaya had to leave her mom and move with her dad from Oakland to LA (about a six-hour drive). She says it was tough—she missed her mom a lot. About two years in, Zendaya was making enough money that her mom could move to LA, too.

If you haven't seen the show (how could you not?), it's a comedy about two likable best friends, CeCe and Rocky, who live in Chicago and audition for a local dance show called "Shake It Up, Chicago!" They're hired to be professional backup dancers, and the show follows their adventures and antics onstage and off, in school and at home. Rocky's a good kid, an overachiever who wants everyone to like her. (Don't we all?) She is pulled into CeCe's crazy schemes, and when she tries to get them both out of trouble, they usually get in deeper.

The show was a huge hit for Disney and its stars. Even when it was canceled after three years, *Shake It Up* was the number one show for children six to eleven and nine to fourteen.

Why so popular? "I think because it's relatable to every kid. I mean, they can all find themselves in one of the characters. They can say, 'Oh I'm a Rocky, Oh I'm a CeCe,'" Zendaya told Clevver TV during the second season.

The show was like a second family for the young actors; everyone was close. They grew up with one another. And in a sense, they grew up with their fans.

Zendaya credits the show with helping her mature and learn about comedy, how to be funny on camera. It's also when she started recording music. With Bella Thorne, she released the single "Watch Me." In 2012 she signed with Hollywood Records, and the following year she released "Replay," which reached number 40 on the *Billboard* Hot 100 chart! A few months later she put out her album, simply titled *Zendaya*, which reached number 41 on the chart.

"I think I kind of always grew up around music. It's always been something that's very important in my family," she told MTV. "My dad, he actually plays the drums, and when I was little I would kinda, like, curl up in a little ball by his drums and I would fall asleep while he was playing. I don't know—it felt, like, warm and comfortable there." #FamilyGoals

Here's the SCOOP! Some of Zendaya's all-time favorite musicians are Michael Jackson, Rascal Flatts, Lauryn Hill, Beyoncé, and Solange. She even had a cameo in Beyoncé's *Lemonade* video!

With two careers, Zendaya was working hard—five days a week on the show plus recording her album. And don't forget school—she wasn't going to an actual school anymore, but she had tutors on set.

And here's an extra SCOOP! In the state of California, child actors ages six to sixteen must be accompanied by a studio teacher on set and are required to do academic work three hours each school day while they're working.

But this isn't the point in the story where our star takes a break or falls apart or joins a religious cult or has some life epiphany. She was just getting started, loving her newfound success. And pretty soon, another opportunity would come her way.

By the time Zendaya was seated across the table from Disney brass to discuss her next project, she was a little older, a little wiser, and a little more woke. And she had more power. Zendaya brought a list of demands—and Disney listened.

They wanted to call the new show *Super Awesome Katy*. "I was like, 'The title is wack. That's gonna change.'" And she rejected the character's name. "Do I look like a Katy to you?" she told *Vogue*. (No, no you don't.) She also insisted that the show feature a family of color. And she demanded some control—she wanted to be one of the show's producers.

Zendaya won on all counts. (The girl's got a head for business.) The show was to be called *K.C. Undercover*, K.C.'s family would be a family of color, and guess who was made a producer?

But that wasn't all she wanted. She had a specific vision for the character.

"I wanted to make sure that she wasn't good at singing or acting or dancing. That she wasn't artistically inclined. I didn't want them to all of a sudden be like, 'Oh, yeah, and then she sings this episode!' No. She can't dance; she can't sing," she told *Vogue*. And there was more. "I want her to be martial arts–trained. I want her to be able to do everything that a guy can do. . . . I want her to be a brainiac." Check, check, and check!

Set in Washington, DC, the show is about K.C. Cooper, a high school math genius whose parents are spies. When K.C. discovers what her parents do, they bring her into the "Organization" to spy with them. The show is about their dangerous missions and their more mundane, suburban family life with her siblings. Like *Shake It Up, K.C. Undercover* had a successful three-season run.

Back to those early meetings, when Zendaya and the show's creators were nailing down the terms of the deal: Zendaya told producers she wanted K.C. to be a normal girl with an extraordinary life.

Sound like anyone you know?

SCOOP! QUIZ

ARE YOU A *SHAKE IT UP* SUPERFAN?

 ⬇ TAKE OUR QUIZ TO FIND OUT! ⬇

1. What does CeCe dare Rocky to do on vacation during a game of "truth or dare" that lands her in the hospital?

_____

2. In the show finale, after she falls, who does CeCe think is her best friend?

_____

3. CeCe has a dream in one episode in which Gary is a food. What food is he?

_____

4. Who is afraid of flying?

_____

5. In the first episode, which character, CeCe or Rocky, doesn't make it onto "Shake It Up, Chicago!" in the beginning?

_____

6. What is CeCe's little brother's name?

_____

7. What is Rocky's real name?

_____

8. What job does CeCe's mom have?

_____

9. Who plays Ty Blue?

_____

10. In the "Future It Up" episode, how many children does Rocky have?

_____

Check your answers on page 93!

CHAPTER 3

THE PERSONAL STUFF

*B*etween show tapings, filming, rehearsals, recordings, press tours, design meetings, photo shoots—you get the idea—chilling is not often an option for Zendaya. What does she do with a rare day off?

"I do nothing. I just stay inside and, like, watch Harry Potter and just, like, don't do anything." If you haven't watched *Vogue*'s "73 Questions with Zendaya," check it out. You won't see much of the house, where she likes to do nothing, but you will get a look at the backyard and pool.

Zendaya told Stephen Colbert that after finishing the first season of *Euphoria*, she turned into a vampire. "I just became nocturnal, and I just stayed up all night and watched a lot of crime documentaries."

Zendaya moved into her own house in Los Angeles when she was twenty. She reportedly paid $1.4 million for it! Her Mediterranean-style crib is pretty sweet: five bedrooms, five bathrooms, a three-car garage, and lemon trees in the backyard. She says it's the first time she's ever had a pool and lived in a place that's so beautiful, so she appreciates it more because she had to work for it. She lives there with her dog, Noon, a miniature schnauzer that was a gift from an ex.

Here's the SCOOP! Noon has his own Twitter account: @nooncoleman

Zendaya knew when she was ready to go out on her own. "I had grown up—I moved out, and it was time for me to be the sole voice in my career and make my own choices," she says. "I just had too many people I was trying to please, too many opinions, and I was constantly talked out of following my gut and my instinct."

Being in charge of her own career was easier to

do in her own space. But she's still tight with her family, and some of them have lived with her. She loves to have family around when she's off from work and doing nothing—just don't ask her to go anywhere.

And she has a special relationship with her mom. Zendaya says Claire has always been and still is her role model. Why? "Because she's a teacher and she's spent her whole life giving and I really admire that," she told *Vogue*'s "73 Questions." Zendaya says she'd like to try teaching someday.

Here's another small SCOOP! Zendaya's mom placed crystals around Zendaya's new house to give it positive energy.

Zendaya's mom undoubtedly admires her daughter. But one thing she doesn't admire? Her driving. A few years ago, mom and daughter made a short video called "Story Time with My Mom," with Claire talking about an accident Zendaya had that tore up the front end of her car. Zendaya blamed it on the curb. Mom wasn't buying that. Nice going, Zendaya!

Aside from driving, whatever she does, Zendaya goes hard. She puts a lot of pressure on herself, always striving to be her best. That can be stressful, and Zendaya says she struggles with anxiety.

"I'm a natural perfectionist and I always want to do the right thing and be the best I possibly can. And I think we're all kind of on a journey learning how to be more patient and more kind to ourselves and allow ourselves the space to exist a little bit."

Maybe all that hard-on-herself, perfectionist stuff stems from being a Virgo. If you don't know much about Virgos, they can be quite particular about the details. Zendaya admits that the most Virgo thing about her is she's a bit of "a control freak." (Relatable!) Virgos are known to be loyal and passionate . . . and sensitive and intense. They're also known to work super hard. And they tend to live an organized life.

Like most celebs, Zendaya has peeps to help her keep it all together. Her personal assistant is a guy named Darnell (another one-namer) who pops up in some of the videos on Zendaya's YouTube channel. What was the most random errand he ever had to do for his boss? Darnell says it was when she asked him to get her Pizza Hut. Here's the catch: The nearest one was a forty-five-minute drive away.

And of course, Zendaya has loads of fashion help. She's got a fab sense of style, but that doesn't all come naturally. Her super creative stylist, Law Roach, is responsible for those savage runway, film premiere, and Met gala looks. (More on Zendaya's fashion later!)

Zendaya knows how to play the diva on the red carpet. But generally speaking, she's pretty low-key. Like no makeup, hair-pulled-on-top-of-her-head-in-a-messy-knot and sweats low-key. She says her go-to out-of-the-house uniform is black pants, white tee. And she loves her Converse.

If you're wondering how she stays fit, it's not the gym. Because she claims she doesn't work out. (Seriously?) She doesn't cook, either—says she's too lazy! Zendaya works so much, sometimes she forgets to eat, but for breakfast she loves to smear Nutella on just about anything. Sometimes she skips a meal and goes straight to ice cream. That's some serious sweet tooth! And she likes fast food, but because she's a vegetarian, she has to be more creative when ordering takeout.

On the subject of genes, it seems that Zendaya is good at just about everything. She sings, she dances, she acts, she designs clothing. But she says not everything comes naturally to her.

"Obviously when you try something, right away it's not always perfect or it's not always great. And I was not great when I started hip-hop dancing. I just was really bad." In the MTV video "The Story of Zendaya," she says, "I wanted to be good, so that's what you do when you really want to learn something: You work hard, you open your mind, and you do it."

Excellent advice!

One thing Zendaya says she's just no good at? Spelling and grammar! And her fans point it out to her all the time on social media. Zendaya says she's greatful (whoops! We mean grateful) for the corrections.

Good to know that she's not perfect!

SCOOP! QUIZ

WHICH ONE WOULD ZENDAYA CHOOSE?

Sleep in pop out of bed?

Wake up grumpy happy?

Shower bath?

Coffee  juice?

Check your answers on page 93!

Soda  water?

Vegetables meat?

Gardenias roses?

To tattoo not to tattoo?

Teleportation invisibility?

Jammin' party playlist or slammin' party outfit?

CHAPTER 4

FROM DANCING WITH THE STARS
TO REWRITING THEM

Shake It Up season three was still a hit when Zendaya decided to shake things up in a new way: she said yes to *Dancing with the Stars*. At sixteen, she was the show's youngest contestant ever at the time. Proof that kids can bring it!

She was paired with Valentin "Val" Chmerkovskiy, a thirty-three-year-old professional dancer, and the duo was a fan fave from the start. And in each dance, Zendaya turned in a professional performance. She had the skills, precision, and grace to pull it off as if she'd been doing the tango, cha-cha, and samba her whole life. How about the Viennese waltz? The paso doble? Piece of cake.

Like everything else she does, she gave 110

percent to her performances; it wasn't just a dance, but a piece of theater. She transformed into a character. And those flapper dresses and gowns were straight fire!

In the pre-performance video for the Argentine tango, Zendaya talks about the challenges of making such a romantic/sexy dance work.

"I'm young, and it's kinda tough when you're talking about, oh, being in love, and all this stuff that I've never experienced or never really understood, in my own personal life."

She not only pulled it off, she slayed! It's a testament to the power of commitment and Zendaya's never-ending supply of talents.

Despite their incredible performances, the duo came in second place—a major disappointment to her young fans. But hey, not bad!

Val told *ET* that second place wasn't good enough. "My biggest heartbreak wasn't winning with Zendaya. That was a huge heartbreak for me because she was sixteen, I wanted this to be such a huge moment for her. She worked so hard and I really wanted her to lift that trophy and jump-start her career." He blames himself and says he could have done better.

Hey, Val, don't sweat it. Look what came next.

There was *K.C. Undercover*, of course. And then in 2017, Zendaya hit the big screen in a big way with two mega movies.

First up: *Spider-Man: Homecoming*.

Zendaya tells *Marie Claire* that when she went to audition for *Spider-Man: Homecoming*, she was concerned they were looking for a white girl. That didn't stop her—but it did affect her pre-audition choices.

"I definitely went into it like, 'Hopefully they'll'—as they call it in the industry—'go ethnic.' I remember making the decision to straighten my hair. I didn't know that they were going to be more diverse in their casting. I didn't know that I was walking into a situation where they were already breaking the rules. You get so used to having to break the rules for people."

She got the part of Michelle "MJ" Jones, whose hair's never straight—it's kind of a mess, which is on-point for her personality. MJ is an outsider, science nerd, and eccentric—a loner who likes to keep an eye on Peter Parker, aka Spider-Man. Most unforgettable Zendaya scene? When she's in detention and the teacher asks what she's doing there. MJ holds up her sketch pad and says, "I just like coming here to sketch people in crisis." Zendaya's got the deadpan delivery down.

Here's the SCOOP! Laura Harrier, one of Zendaya's costars in the movie, says Zendaya was so popular with fans that people would come up to her, crying, when the two actors would get their nails done in Atlanta. (They shot for weeks in Georgia.)

MJ has a bigger role in *Spider-Man: Far from Home*. But Zendaya took center stage with Spider-Man star Tom Holland in a very different kind of venue before number two came out. Have you seen the costars duke it out on *Lip Sync Battle*? If you haven't, you've gotta check it out. Seriously. It is objectively one of the most epic YouTube moments of the twenty-first century.

In the second round, Zendaya channels Bruno Mars's look and vibe: lip syncing and dancing to "24K Magic." She's got the red shorts-suit and baseball cap. Supes cute! And she's got the moves to match—including pop & lock.

But Tom Holland, well, his take on Rihanna's "Umbrella" is iconic. Against any other opponent, Zendaya would have won. No doubt. But she really didn't stand a chance once Holland threw down. Her face is priceless as she watches him, dressed as Rihanna, rain falling on the stage. He even ends it with a flip. The man has serious dance skills and commits! (He is a trained dancer, and he did play Billy Elliot in the musical about a child dancer when he was a kid.)

Both actors say it was one of the most stressful things they've ever done.

She may not have won, but after the battle, *Lip Sync* host LL Cool J said of Zendaya, "She's cool. You can manufacture fame. You can manufacture publicity. You can manufacture songs. You can't manufacture cool."

Here's the double SCOOP! That lip sync battle got Bruno Mars's attention, and he put her in his video for "Versace on the Floor."

What's cooler than a triple threat? Try quadruple threat. Zendaya doesn't just act, sing, and dance in *The Greatest Showman*, she flies through the air!

> **"I never thought that I would be doing any type of acrobatic trapeze work in my life."**

Zendaya is gorgeous and graceful as the trapeze artist Anne Wheeler, who falls in love with Zac Efron's character, Philip Carlyle, in the movie musical about circus owner P. T. Barnum. She makes it look effortless, again, as if she's been doing it forever.

The scene with Efron, the two of them singing "Rewrite the Stars" while flying through the air, is so romantic. And that electric kiss between the star-crossed lovers—wow!

"This might be my favorite kiss, I think ever," Efron said during a press tour for the movie.

Wait—did he say ever? No "onscreen" qualifier? Hmmm . . . Zendaya gives a "What?" look to the camera when he says it. He does go on to talk about the characters' relationship, but you know, who's hearing anything after that?

Zendaya says since you have to wait so long for that kiss, there's a big payoff. Uh-huh.

And here's the triple **SCOOP!** Zendaya stopped that press interview for a moment to fix the reporter's hair so he wouldn't be upset when he watched the interview back. Love that.

Rehearsals weren't always smooth. "It was a lot of training, a lot of slamming into each other sometimes, a lot of not doing it right, but at the end of the day, it turned out pretty great," Zendaya told the hosts of *Today*. Yeah it did!

The relationship between Anne and Philip is particularly moving because it's taboo: A romance between a black woman and a white man was a non-starter in the nineteenth century. "It was a forbidden love, something that was not supposed to happen. I think that's what's special about these two characters," Zendaya says. "It's the constant battle of mind and heart, you know?"

The message? She says it's to always allow your heart to speak louder and love who you want to love.

That's a message to hold on to—like, for life!

Before we dive into Zendaya's love life, let's take a quick SCOOP! stroll—or should we say foxtrot—into some ballroom dancing styles.

SCOOP! EXTRA

THOSE PESKY BALLROOM DANCING TERMS

Wondering what a paso doble is? We got you.

1. **SAMBA:** A Brazilian style of dance that dates back to the early 1900s. It was introduced to the U.S. when Fred Astaire and Dolores del Río danced the carioca in the movie *Flying Down to Rio.*

2. **CHA-CHA:** Originated in Cuba in the 1950s and is derived from the rumba and the mambo. The name cha-cha imitates the shuffling sounds of the dancers' feet.

3. **JIVE:** Created by African Americans in the U.S. during the 1930s, jive was brought to the public's attention by musician Cab Calloway. Jive is a happy, energetic dance, and in competitions it is performed at 176 beats per minute.

4 PASO DOBLE (pronounced: PAH-so DOE-blay): Means "double-step" in Spanish. It's one of the most dramatic of the Latin dances.

5 TANGO: This dance originated in Argentina and involves movements that can be slow and stalking, or sharp and staccato. Also a very dramatic style of dance.

6 FOXTROT: A smooth dance with continuous, flowing movements across the floor. It is danced to big band music, usually with vocals. It originated in the U.S. in the early 1900s.

7 WALTZ (from the German "Walzen"): The waltz originated in Austria as early as the seventeenth century. It is danced in 3/4 time.

HERE'S THE SCOOP!

ON P. T. BARNUM

Born in 1810, P. T. (Phineas Taylor) Barnum was an American showman and businessman who turned the circus into a three-ring spectacle. Played by Hugh Jackman, *The Greatest Showman* paints him as a sympathetic character. But Barnum, who started out as a newspaperman and later became a politician, was infamous for hoaxes and exploiting vulnerable people and animals, making him a controversial figure. He was also a great success. With his partner, James Bailey, he created a traveling show that would one day merge with the Ringling Brothers circus and be called "Ringling Brothers and Barnum and Bailey Circus," aka "The Greatest Show on Earth." It became the most enduring circus in American history; it closed for good in 2017.

CHAPTER 5

ZENDAYA'S LEADING MEN AND LEADING LOVES

*I*f this were SCOOP!'s Taylor Swift bio (don't forget to check it out!), this chapter would be a lengthy one. But this is going to be one of the shorter chapters in this book. Sorry to disappoint.

Zendaya likes to say that her fans really know her. Maybe so. But how much do you really know about her love life? She's been adept at keeping most of it a secret.

Did you know she had a boyfriend for four years, from sometime in 2013 to the spring of 2017? That means she was seventeen to twenty-one or so when they were dating.

He's the dude who gifted her Noon, the dog.

She calls him her "first love."

Shortly after First Love gave her Noon, he broke up with her. Say what? Who would even dare? Well, this unnamed fool did.

Here's the SCOOP! Fans and media speculation have pointed to Zendaya's friend Trevor Jackson as the guy in question, but she has always denied it.

"It wasn't a good ending," Zendaya told *Vogue* in a much-reported interview. "You know you're OK in a breakup when your first thought is not, What did I do wrong?" she says. "It's, That was the dumbest decision of your life, and you're going to regret it forever." So healthy.

Kinda thinking First Love's gotta realize that breaking up with Zendaya was the dumbest decision of his life and he is going to regret it forever, right?

Moving on . . .

You know the rumors about Zendaya and Tom Holland, her Spider-Man costar? The media, and fans, love to fantasize that onscreen romantics are off-screen lovers too. (Think Bradley Cooper and Lady Gaga.) These two say they were never an item. Just great friends. Maybe they're telling the truth, maybe not. Maybe they were once together, but not likely anymore. Holland has been seen looking very cozy with a British woman named Olivia Bolton, and he's reportedly smitten, so there's that.

But still, a little analysis is in order, 'cause Zendaya and Holland are sooo cute onscreen. And you'd like to think that maybe they did date, once upon a time.

✔ Chemistry? Check. You feel it in the movies, you feel it on shows like *Lip Sync Battle* and *Jimmy Kimmel Live!* when they're guests together.

✔ Good match? Check. They're both actors hitting their stride with hectic schedules.

✔ Sense of humor? Check. They both have a healthy one.

✓ **Is he good enough for our queen? Well, that's a tough one. But, check. He's known to be a good guy. And he's British—so extra points for the accent. He's mad talented. Oh, and those dance moves!**

A "source" told *People* magazine that Zendaya and Holland started dating when they were filming *Spider-Man: Homecoming.* According to the source, they took secret vacations together. Zendaya clapped back on Instagram with "Wait wait . . . my favorite is when it says we go on vacations together HA! I haven't been on a vacation in years!"

Other than that, the receipts just aren't there.

Zendaya has also been linked to *Euphoria* cast member Jacob Elordi. But here we go again. Rumors swirled like a soft-serve SCOOP! when fans spotted them in the back of a tourist pic and then again at the movies in Sherman Oaks, Cali. Back in December 2019, they were supposedly spotted together and cozy in Australia. Here's the catch: She was there for work—receiving the *GQ Australia* Woman of the Year award—and he was there for the awards as well. And he is Australian.

Elordi told *GQ Australia*, "Zendaya is an amazing creative, you know? She's super dope to work with. She's an incredible artist and a very caring person to all of us." And then he said, wait for it . . . she's like a sister to him. Talk about letting the air out of a story with one pin.

Anyway, Elordi recently dated actress Joey King and was later linked to model Cari Flowers.

What about Zac Efron? There doesn't seem to be any traction there. But that kiss! If anything, it sure looked like he was crushing on her in those press interviews. Check out his expression when he looks at her or talks about that scene. But Zac was linked with Danish Olympic swimmer Sarah Bro in late 2019. And then there were the Lily Collins rumors.

What about Odell Beckham Jr., you ask? The rumors about Zendaya and the NFL star go back to 2016 when the two were spotted at a New York Knicks game. She had fun with it—in a video about how they bumped into each other. "Folks, people will think we planned this. I didn't know he was coming tonight." She was with her mom, by the way, and Zendaya pointed out that Claire and Odell were sporting the same blond hair.

"Literally if I show up anywhere with anyone that automatically happens," Zendaya told *Extra* of the media frenzy that followed the game.

Fast forward to 2019 when she snuck up behind Beckham at the airport in Paris. They hugged and the rumors fired up all over again. As usual, just not enough to go on, folks!

This one is leaving you unsatisfied, right? The woman is really good at keeping it all on the down-low. What more can we say?

SCOOP! EXTRA

WHO SHOULD ZENDAYA DATE?

Who do you want to see Zendaya with? Circle your answer below!

TIMOTHÉE CHALAMET
Born: December 27, 1995
Sign: Capricorn

AUSTIN ABRAMS
Born: September 2, 1996
Sign: Virgo

JOHN BOYEGA
Born: March 17, 1992
Sign: Pisces

KEITH POWERS
Born: August 22, 1992
Sign: Leo

NOAH CENTINEO
Born: May 9, 1996
Sign: Taurus

ANSEL ELGORT
Born: March 14, 1994
Sign: Pisces

CHAPTER 6

EUPHORIA: FAR FROM HOME

One of the longest distances Zendaya has ever traveled—maybe *the* longest—is from Disney to HBO and *Euphoria*. The series is a complete 180 from *Shake It Up* and *K.C. Undercover*. In a word, it's intense.

It happens—in every Disney star's life (see the Jonas Brothers, Miley Cyrus, etc.). There comes a time to do more mature material, whether it's their song choices or TV and film roles. Disney stars often look back and recall how, at a certain age, they began to feel stifled and needed to take on more adult roles.

Zendaya has grown up and out of those Disney roles. But she seems to have skipped that super angsty phase that plagues so many child stars. She does, however, play someone with a serious drug problem on *Euphoria*.

So, how did it all happen?

"I'd been working on something consistently since I was, like, thirteen years old, and so it was the first time where I just had a big space and I didn't know what I was going to do, and everything I read, nothing really spoke to me or pulled—I was looking for, like, a feeling," she told Stephen Colbert. "And I read *Euphoria*, and I just, I don't know, I couldn't quite explain it, but I cared so deeply for the character of Rue and I felt connected to her. And then I met Sam [Levinson], who's our creator and our writer, and I then understood that a lot of what Rue is is him."

Rue is so much more than a girl addicted to drugs. And that's in large part due to Zendaya's portrayal. Zendaya's Rue is a fully realized high school student, a young person with difficult and sometimes life-threatening problems, but someone who is truly likable. And you can empathize with her. She's struggling not only with addiction, but with anxiety, depression, and the grief of losing her father. Maybe you can understand what she's going through—maybe you can only understand some of it or maybe it's all very foreign and scary. But you can still feel for her because Zendaya has created a sympathetic character.

The show was a major leap for Zendaya. The acting is a monumental shift from playing K.C., and Zendaya says the series really pushes her. But the payoff? Totally worth it.

"It's the most exciting, exhausting, but fulfilling thing I've ever done," she told *Vogue* on "73 Questions."

Euphoria is about teens, but it's not a show for kids or, many would argue, teens—a lot of teens and their parents would find it disturbing and graphic. It's rough: *Euphoria* tackles difficult topics and doesn't shy away from scenes that can be upsetting to watch. Some critics have complained that the sex and violence are gratuitous: that it's an unrealistic depiction of high school.

Most media critics agree on one thing: Zendaya gives a strong performance in this show, and she's come quite a long way from her Disney days.

Zendaya has worked hard to get the character right. And it shows, in spades. In the end, she says Rue is a mixture of her and Sam Levinson, their issues, their personality traits, what they have in common, and what they don't. Levinson writes from experience: He's a recovered addict. Zendaya says Rue feels real to her as a result.

The camera gives you an up close and personal window into Rue's life, and her face, which is so expressive in this show. You can see the pain in her eyes and the sheer joy in her smile on the rare occasions when she's truly happy. And there's something poignant and real in her relationship with her *Euphoria* mom, played by Nika Williams, and her little sister, played by Storm Reid.

Rue's sparks of happiness come from her friendship with Jules, another lead character on the show. Jules is a transgender girl, played by trans actor Hunter Schafer. She has an ethereal quality and she's different from anyone Rue has ever met. The two instantly click and become tight. But Jules can also be a source of pain for Rue, and the friendship/romance isn't always easy or clearly defined.

Here's the SCOOP! Zendaya and Hunter, who didn't know each other before *Euphoria*, say they've gotten super close in real life because of the show.

Theirs isn't the only relationship that's examined in *Euphoria*. There are other friendships and some dysfunctional romantic storylines. Jacob Elordi's violent character, Nate, and Alexa Demie's character, Maddy, are in a terribly destructive relationship that they just can't seem to quit.

"Rue has such a darkness to her, but also an

innocence. I have to be super vulnerable and sad in front of people. It's weird, but cathartic in a lot of ways," Zendaya told *Elle.*

Translation: Zendaya has to cry a lot on camera. And she says she hates to cry in front of people.

"I always hide my face when I cry," she told *Elle.* "I would cover up my whole performance with my hands if I let myself."

She says it's been a little scary to put herself out there like that.

Here's the double SCOOP!
Zendaya and Labrinth recorded a song that features prominently in the *Euphoria* **season finale, "All for Us." Check it out!**

What does she hope viewers get from the show? "I hope they feel something, you know? Like, whatever that is—I don't know. I just hope they feel something," she told *Vogue*'s "73 Questions."

What does she get out of it besides mad props for her performances and a paycheck? She's become extremely close to the cast and crew, some of whom call her "Z." (She invited the entire cast to her home for Thanksgiving.)

And it's been a bit like therapy. "I think *Euphoria* taught me a lot about myself. It made me more confident in my own abilities, because I doubted myself a lot."

It's hard to believe Zendaya has ever doubted herself, but it goes to show you stars have insecurities, even when they belong to the Marvel Universe.

Just a week after *Euphoria* debuted, in June 2019, *Spider-Man: Far from Home* opened. It was Zendaya's second foray into superhero territory, and this time, she had a more prominent role.

MJ is still MJ in *Far from Home*; she's whip smart and quirky. On the red carpet at the movie's premiere, Zendaya was asked what she and MJ have in common. "I still think we connect on the awkwardness, I think I'm still also trying to figure out how to talk to people that I like, so I can relate to her on that. But also I just think our want to be alone, I guess, to be honest, is that sad?" Not at all, Z! You be you.

As the film opens, Peter Parker tells best friend Ned that he's got a thing for MJ. But in the next moment, she sees them and says, "What up, dorks?" Doesn't look like much chance for romance.

Far from Home is set mostly in Europe, where Peter and his classmates are on a school trip. Of course, trouble finds Peter in Venice, Prague, and London, and he reluctantly answers the call to save the world. But his first priority is telling MJ that he really likes her.

SCOOP! SPOILER ALERT
Don't read on if you haven't seen the movie.

It starts to look like MJ is into Peter, too—but as is usual for the boy superhero, he disappears when she's just about to get close to him. The awkwardness between them is always palpable. The thing is, she's got him figured out and backs him into a corner, asking if he's Spider-Man. After his initial denials, he confesses when duty calls.

Finally, after he's saved London from total annihilation . . . what he's been waiting for, what we've all been waiting and pining for, that kiss happens. And it's introverted MJ who makes the first move.

Who wouldn't want to go out with MJ? Okay, she's awkward. But she's funny. And honest to a fault. Not to mention adorable. No makeup, hair pulled into a messy ponytail, a few inches taller than our superhero. (She's 5'10", he's 5'8".) And she gives off serious loyalty vibes.

Is there another *Spider-Man* in Zendaya's future? Certainly seems possible.

But first, let's take this moment for a little pop quiz! Pencils out! (No googling, either!)

HOW *MARVELOUS* ARE YOU?

1. Name the primary creator of Marvel characters, who has cameos in Marvel films.

_____

2. On what continent is Wakanda?

_____

3. What fruit is Pepper Potts allergic to?

_____

4. Who is the villain in *Ant-Man and the Wasp*?

_____

5. Which Marvel character does Chris Evans play?

_____

6. How many Marvel films has Tony Stark appeared in?

_____

7. What is Star-Lord/Peter Quill's mother's name?

_____

8. Who plays Thanos in the Avengers movies?

_____

9. Without his suit, does Tony Stark have superpowers?

_____

10. What fictional metal is Thor's hammer made of?

_____

11. Which Marvel character does Scarlett Johansson play?

_____

12. How many original Avengers are there? Give yourself an extra point if you can name them.

_____

13. Name Tony Stark's first robot assistant. Give yourself an extra point if you know what the letters of his name stand for.

_____

14. What is Captain America's shield made of?

_____

15. What does Aunt May call that "spidey sense" Peter Parker gets? Hint: He doesn't like it.

_____

Check your answers on page 94!

CHAPTER 7

THE SHAPE-SHIFTER

She walked into the 2019 Met Gala in a voluminous but drab gray ball gown, wearing a short blond wig. She was clearly channeling Cinderella. But after she made her entrance and posed for the cameras, her stylist, dressed in a hooded blue coat, waved a magic wand, and voilà! The dress lit up from bottom to top. It was spectacular! The Tommy Hilfiger gown was a feat of technical wizardry and a showstopper. The theme for the Met Gala that year was "Camp: Notes on Fashion," and Zendaya was on point: She delivered the camp, in spades, and of course the fairy-tale beauty.

Here's the SCOOP! Zendaya even dropped a glass slipper as she entered the event!

Zendaya's stylist, Law Roach, calls them moments: you know, those iconic, savage shots of Zendaya slaying the red carpet at the Met Gala or a movie premiere, taking Hollywood glamour to the next level. It's not just a look they're going for, but the creation of a memorable character. Zendaya's a chameleon, a shape-shifter, thanks to Roach's vision and her own sense of adventure and daring. Her hair changes with the wind (and wigs) and her look migrates from David Bowie to Cinderella with a tap of Roach's wand.

Like Cinderella, Zendaya's look goes through magical transformations from one event to another. And it's not always about achieving beauty. Zendaya and Roach like to say their mantra is "We don't do pretty. Pretty is boring." Noted! But when has Zendaya ever been out in public looking anything less than pretty?

Even in her more costumey moments, Zendaya is always pretty. Wait—that's an understatement. It's more like gorgeous, ethereal, stunning. And totally glam . . . Every. Single. Time. That butterfly dress at the Australian premiere of *The Greatest Showman*? Truly phenomenal! (And one of the star's favorites.)

As Saint Joan of Arc at yet another Met Gala (see a theme here?) she wore her hair cropped with bangs, wavy, and rusty red. The Versace silver metallic dress was extraordinary and battle ready: It featured an armored neck and shoulder piece—aka a pauldron—and a spiked belt.

"I love to slay a red carpet," she told *Allure*. "When I step on one, I'm a different person," she said, "like Sasha Fierce and Beyoncé." Done and done!

She is as tall and willowy as a supermodel and possesses the sweetest smile, one of her front teeth charmingly askew. But like her clothing, Zendaya's face shows a wide range of moods—she can read girlish at one turn, the ultimate diva at another. And those eyebrows! They're fabulous and so expressive. Zendaya says she prefers them that way. When she was thirteen, she had them done and hated how thin they were. They've been big and bold ever since.

One of Zendaya's fashion choices early on landed her in a bit of a media whirlwind. At the 2015 Oscars, when she was eighteen, Zendaya wore a white Vivienne Westwood gown fit for a goddess. She also donned long locs—not hers, but you would never know. *Fashion Police* host Giuliana Rancic took notice, and what should have been a lovely moment for an up-and-coming young actress took on the whiff of racism with her comments. Rancic said Zendaya must have smelled of "patchouli" and "weed." Hol' up!

Zendaya clapped back on Instagram and won the day. "There is a fine line between what is funny and disrespectful," she wrote. "Someone said something about my hair at the Oscars that left me in awe. Not because I was relishing in rave outfit reviews, but because I was hit with ignorant slurs and pure disrespect."

The post was long and thoughtful, and she added,

"To say that an 18 year old young woman with locs must smell of patchouli oil or 'weed' is not only a large stereotype but outrageously offensive. I don't usually feel the need to respond to negative things but certain remarks cannot go unchecked."

She sparked a national conversation about hair, race, and racism with her posts. And women sent her photos of their own locs in solidarity. She says it was empowering. But ultimately, it was Zendaya and celebrity supporters like Ava DuVernay, Rosie Perez, Whoopi Goldberg, and Terry McMillan who empowered women of color everywhere.

Here's a small SCOOP! Mattel created a Zendaya Barbie modeled after that look!

Rancic apologized and said she learned a lot about how much damage stereotypes and clichés can do.

Despite the controversy, that white dress was

hot. But if we're talking *the* hottest dress she ever wore, here's one vote for the custom emerald silk gown with sheer bustier top by Vera Wang that Zendaya wore to the 2019 Emmy Awards. Fashion pundits said she was channeling the supervillain Poison Ivy. Killer!

About all those ever-changing hairstyles . . . sometimes it's her hair, sometimes it's not. "So many people get stressed out every time I wear a different hairstyle on the red carpet," she once explained in an Insta video. "It's called a wig, people. Say it with me: 'W-I-G: *wiiiiiiiig.*'"

Does she have tattoos? Nah. Zendaya says she loves them, but she doesn't want one—at least not now. On *Euphoria*, her character Rue and her best friend Jules get "Rules" tattooed on the inside of their bottom lips. (Ouch.) Zendaya says she and Hunter Schafer, who plays Jules, have toyed with the idea of getting the same tattoo in real life.

What's the most overworn item in her closet? Her Converse.

The most luxe thing she ever wore? "I went to a premiere, and I had these earrings—they were big, beautiful earrings, and I thought they were fake to be honest with you," she told *Vogue*'s "73 Questions." "And then there was this article that came out the next day that was like, 'Zendaya wears million-dollar earrings,' and I was like, 'Law, did you put me in million-dollar earrings last night?' And he was like, 'Hm, probably.'" Unfortunately, she didn't get to keep them.

Zendaya's love of fashion led her from *Vogue* cover girl into the fashion design business. She started a shoe and clothing line called Daya. But things didn't go so well—the company was plagued by complaints. She fired the company producing clothing for Daya with apologies to her fans and is now collaborating with her Cinderella dress designer, Tommy Hilfiger.

It's a partnership made in '70s fashion heaven, with bold mix, match, and clash prints; wide legs; and a touch of Hollywood glam. You know those printed, fitted pantsuits you've seen Zendaya wearing on her Insta and in magazine ads? The ones that give her legs for days? Those are from the TOMMYXZENDAYA collection.

One thing Zendaya insisted on in her collaboration with Hilfiger was including plus sizes in their line. He hadn't made them before.

"That was my thing—I'm not going to make clothes my sister or my niece or any of the women in my family can't wear," she says. "A lot of the clothes were for tall people, too. For my mom, this is the first time she can wear pants and not get them altered—she's six feet four." Aw—love that. And wow, Claire!

Zendaya has a partnership with another powerhouse—the French cosmetics company Lancôme. She was named the brand's latest global ambassador in 2019, and stars in a commercial for the fragrance Idôle. With Zendaya riding a horse through the streets of LA to the soundtrack of Sia's "Unstoppable," her hair a flowing mane behind her, it's a dramatic ad. She looks stunning and powerful. And yes, unstoppable.

Asked about her idols in a behind-the-scenes Lancôme interview, Zendaya said, "I always say my idol is my future self. I don't know who she is yet, I haven't met her yet, but I know she's there and she's waiting for me in the future."

The future is calling, and it features Zendaya wearing a hot pink Tom Ford breastplate, aka shirt. Have you seen it? It's literally *the* definition of fire.

FASHION EXTRA: EXTRAORDINARY
WOMEN OF COLOR

When Zendaya and Tommy Hilfiger launched their collaborative clothing line TOMMYNOW in Paris in spring 2019, the fashion world took notice. In addition to the beautiful clothes, the show featured more than fifty models, all of them black women. And not just any models: They ranged in age from eighteen to seventy and included music legend Grace Jones and legendary models Veronica Webb, Beverly Johnson, and Pat Cleveland. Jones, who is seventy, walked the catwalk in a bodysuit, metallic jacket, and boots, looking like a twenty-something. If you're not familiar with the other women, they are trailblazers. Johnson is the first black woman to grace the cover of *Vogue* magazine, in the 1970s. Webb is the first black woman to have a cosmetic contract, with Revlon. And Cleveland is one of the first black women to become a runway and print model. Her career started in the 1960s when a *Vogue* staffer saw the stylish teen on an NYC subway platform. They're all women to whom Zendaya feels indebted for paving the way for herself and other women of color in the business.

CHAPTER 8

A WOMAN WITH A VOICE

Zendaya knows she has a unique platform, and she's all in.

"There's literally injustice happening every second. It's intense and it's overwhelming, and I think a lot of young people are feeling that," she told *Allure*. "But what do we do about it? All I can say is try to find a balance between doing the work and still not letting it destroy you as a person and destroy your hope and faith in humanity."

That's heavy. But Zendaya has always felt a sense of responsibility to her fans and to the world. And maybe that's most noticeable when she talks about women of color in Hollywood, and children of color who aspire to Hollywood. She's talked about the women who came before her (like Beverly Johnson) making it possible for her to find a path in entertainment. But she says the media representation has to be passed on.

"That's the only way doors are going to continue to be open—if we keep inviting people that look like us, and other people who don't look like us, to come through the door," she told *Allure*.

How does that thinking manifest itself? In going for roles that aren't originally intended for women of color, in speaking out in interviews and giving pointed awards speeches, in social media posts like the one on Instagram supporting Colin Kaepernick, and in insisting to Disney that K.C. Cooper's family had to be black. It's called courage and conviction.

Here's the SCOOP! Zendaya's partner in design, Tommy Hilfiger, says she has the heart of an activist. She says it's nice to hear people call her that, but she doesn't see herself that way and she wants to do more.

Zendaya says she is what you might call Hollywood's "acceptable version of a black girl."

At Beautycon 2018 she said, "As a black woman, as a light-skinned black woman, it's important that I'm using my privilege, my platform, to show you how much beauty there is in the African American community."

And just because she might be "acceptable" to Hollywood doesn't mean she always fits roles that are prescribed as one race or another. Her mother explained it this way: "You're not white enough to be white, and you're not black enough to be black." But Zendaya never lets that stop her from auditioning for roles she wants.

Other issues that fire her up? Climate change deniers. Gentrification. Police brutality against black men. It's something she worries about, having a black father and black brothers and nephews. And it's something that makes her feel helpless.

Even back in 2012, Zendaya was doing philanthropic work. She was named an ambassador for Convoy of Hope, a religious organization that does disaster relief work and feeds poor people around the world. In 2013, she recorded a cover of John Legend's "All of Me" to raise money for the organization. Sometimes she uses her birthday to raise money. For her eighteenth, she hosted a fundraiser in alliance with feedONE (part of Convoy of Hope) to feed malnourished children in Haiti, Tanzania, and the Philippines.

When she turned nineteen, Zendaya raised money with CrowdRise to support victims of AIDS and their families in South Africa after taking a trip there and hearing stories about young people dying of AIDS.

And when she turned twenty, she raised $50,000 for Convoy of Hope's Women's Empowerment initiative! Her goal? To help women break the cycle of poverty. Go, Z, go!

Bottom line: Zendaya is an awesome role model for young people, for anyone really. She uses her fame to spread positive messages and raise money for those in need. She tries to support other women and people of color.

She says she wants to be part of the change: of making Hollywood more diverse, and raising awareness about issues of race, poverty, and climate change, to name a few.

Some people—for example, certain politicians—like to lecture celebrities about staying in their lane, to keep quiet about the issues. But Zendaya disagrees. "It's important that creatives of all races, if they have an opportunity or platform, use it to make room for other people."

That's pretty dope, as she might say.

THE QUOTABLE ZENDAYA

From the sublime to the purely practical, Zendaya has a lot to say. Here's some inspiration and advice from a woman who believes you CAN have it all.

"Confidence takes time. A lot of people would be like, 'Why don't you just love yourself?' or 'Why don't you just feel better?' That stuff is much easier said than done."

"I think it's very important to be self-motivated and active in your own career. Every day is a day that you could be getting closer to what you love to do."

"Take your makeup off before you go to bed. I'm serious! Even if you're tired, do it."

"Women are very powerful, and I think we're more powerful together than separated."

"It's allowing yourself to be angry enough to want to be motivated to do something, but not to where it breaks you down."

"If you want the party to jump off . . . play 'This Is How We Do It.' It works every time."

"I don't like the idea that you have to box yourself in or stay in one lane. Why wouldn't I try to make the most of my talents and gifts while I can?"

ZENDAYA'S AWARDS

Zendaya has been nominated for tons of awards, and she's won a lot of them. (Still waiting on an Emmy or Oscar!)

- ⭐ 2014 Radio Disney Music Awards: Best Style

- ⭐ 2014 Teen Choice Awards: Candie's Style Icon

- ⭐ 2016 Nickelodeon Kids' Choice Awards: Favorite Female TV Star for *K.C. Undercover*

- ⭐ 2017 Teen Choice Awards: Choice Summer Movie Actress for *Spider-Man: Homecoming*

- ⭐ 2018 Nickelodeon Kids' Choice Awards: Favorite Movie Actress for *Spider-Man: Homecoming* and *The Greatest Showman*

- ⭐ 2018 Teen Choice Awards: Choice Movie Actress: Drama for *The Greatest Showman*

- ⭐ 2018 Teen Choice Awards: Choice Movie Ship (shared with Zac Efron) for *The Greatest Showman*

- ⭐ 2018 Teen Choice Awards: Choice Collaboration (shared with Zac Efron) for "Rewrite the Stars"

⭐ **2019 Teen Choice Awards: Choice Summer Movie Actress for *Spider-Man: Far from Home***

⭐ **2019 People's Choice Awards: The Female Movie Star of 2019 for *Spider-Man: Far from Home***

⭐ **2019 People's Choice Awards: The Drama TV Star of 2019 for *Euphoria***

⭐ **2020 Satellite Awards: Best Actress—Television Series Drama for *Euphoria***

Okay, so those are just some of the awards she's racked up in the last six years. What will the next six years have in store for Zendaya?

CHAPTER 9

WHAT'S ON DECK?

Chillin' and bingeing crime docs might not be in the cards for Zendaya for a while with *Euphoria* renewed for a second season. That's a many-months-long commitment.

Zendaya's also got a movie coming in 2020 that's already getting hyped by sci-fi fanatics. It'll be a remake of the 1984 film *Dune*, based on the 1965 epic novel of the same name by Frank Herbert. The reboot will be in theaters December 2020.

Dune, which started shooting in March 2019, is directed by Denis Villeneuve (*Blade Runner 2049*, *Arrival*) and stars Timothée Chalamet, Josh Brolin, Stellan Skarsgård, and Rebecca Ferguson. Zendaya will play Chani, the main character's love interest.

The plot: It's 10191 on the dangerous desert

planet Arrakis, the only place in the universe where the valuable spice "melange" can be found. This spice has the power to extend human life and give people superhuman levels of thought, among other things. That's the setup for a major battle to control the sandy planet and its coveted resource.

Sounds exciting! Especially if you're a sci-fier.

Here's the **SCOOP!** Look out, Spider-Man fans: A sequel is reportedly in the works for release in 2021! That's according to IMDb. And looks like the Holland/Zendaya duo will be back! Another two hours of MJ and Peter Parker? Yes, please!

In 2018, there was word that Zendaya would be costarring with Ansel Elgort and a *Spider-Man: Far from Home* costar, Jake Gyllenhaal, in a crime drama called *Finest Kind*. Details are sketchy. But it's reportedly a mobster movie set in Boston with the men playing brothers. And with Zendaya playing opposite Elgort, this could be a big SCOOP! of deliciousness.

Also in 2018, it was announced that Zendaya would be producing and starring in a movie called *A White Lie*. But there hasn't been much info about it since. *A White Lie* is the true story of a woman named Anita Hemmings, who passed as white and became the first black woman to graduate from Vassar College, which in the late 1800s was the country's most prestigious college for women.

Sounds like the perfect project for Zendaya! Here's hoping it happens.

Zendaya has also said she'd like to play Angela Davis in a movie. Davis, who was born in 1944, is a famous African American political activist, academic, and author of books about prison reform, class, and feminism.

Outside the realm of film, Zendaya says she'd like to earn a law degree—not so much to practice law but to better understand her contracts. Could be useful. And time consuming!

The future looks full and fabulous for Zendaya!
Stay tuned.

But first, it's time for a quick SCOOP! quiz . . .

Pencils out!

ULTIMATE ZENDAYA QUIZ

1. In what movie does Zendaya play a yeti? Give yourself an extra point if you can name the singer in the "Zendaya Is Meechee" video.

_____

2. Zendaya was a guest judge on a reality TV series. What is the show called?

_____

3. Zendaya is a brand ambassador for the cosmetic brand Lancôme. She's been the face of another cosmetic company. What is it?

_____

4. On *Dancing with the Stars*, Zendaya and Val were runners-up. Who won season sixteen?

_____

5. What's Zendaya's dog's name?

_____

6. Who did Zendaya play in the Disney TV movie _Frenemies_?

_____

7. In her _Lip Sync Battle_ with Tom Holland, what artist and song did she perform in the first round?

_____

8. Zendaya appeared on three episodes of _The OA_. What was her character's name?

_____

9. On Twitter, Zendaya wrote: "You know, you can live and not _____."
Fill in the blank.

10. What magazine named Zendaya woman of the year in 2019?

_____

11. Zendaya often makes fun of the way she and her father walk. What does she call their walking style?

_____

12. In what city was Zendaya born?

_____

13. When is Zendaya's birthday?

_____

14. What game does the cast of _Spider-Man: Far from Home_ play off-screen, on set?

_____

15. If Zendaya wasn't an actor/singer, what career might she have chosen?

_____

16. What is Zendaya's character's name in _Spider-Man: Homecoming_?

_____

17. Zendaya was once a featured performer in a Kidz Bop video. What was the song?

_____

18. Zendaya appeared in one episode of an ABC sitcom in 2015. Name the show. Give yourself an extra point if you know her character's name.

_____

19. Zendaya is the voice of a video game character. Name the game and character.

_____

20. In 2013, Zendaya was the voice of Lollipop in what direct-to-DVD film?

_____

21. What beauty item does Zendaya always wear?

_____

22. In what city does MJ ask Peter Parker if he's Spider-Man in _Spider-Man: Far from Home_?

_____

23. On what London landmark do MJ and Spider-Man first kiss?

_____

24. What song does Zendaya sing in _Smallfoot_?

_____

25. Where do Philip and Anne (Zac Efron and Zendaya) run into Philip's parents in _The Greatest Showman_?

_____

Check your answers on page 94!

WRITE YOUR OWN SCOOP!

You run into Zendaya in a coffee shop, and she invites you to join her. What three questions do you ask her, and why?

1 _____

_____

_____

2 _____

_____

_____

3 _____

_____

_____

ANSWER KEY

MATCH THESE ONE-NAME CELEBRITIES WITH THEIR SURNAMES

1. Graham, 2. Sebert, 3. Winfrey, 4. Adkins,
5. Moore, 6. Raymond, 7. Ciccone, 8. Fenty,
9. Jones, 10. Yelich-O'Connor, 11. Nelson,
12. Ripoll

ARE YOU A *SHAKE IT UP* SUPERFAN?

1. Swim in the lake, 2. Tinka, 3. A dancing hot
dog, 4. Rocky, 5. CeCe, 6. Flynn, 7. Raquel,
8. Police officer, 9. Roshon Fegan, 10. One

Scoring:
1–3 correct answers: You need dance lessons
4–7 correct answers: You're a backup dancer
8–10 correct answers: You deserve the
spotlight!

WHICH ONE WOULD ZENDAYA CHOOSE?

1. Sleep in, 2. Happy, 3. Shower, 4. Juice,
5. Neither, 6. Vegetables, 7. Gardenias, 8. Not,
9. Teleportation, 10. Playlist

HOW *MARVEL*OUS ARE YOU?

1. Stan Lee, 2. Africa, 3. Strawberries, 4. Ghost,
5. Captain America, 6. Eleven, 7. Meredith,
8. Josh Brolin, 9. No, 10. Uru, 11. Black Widow,
12. Six—*Iron Man, Captain America, Black Widow, Thor, Hulk*, and *Hawkeye*
13. J.A.R.V.I.S.—Just A Rather Very Intelligent System, 14. Vibranium, 15. The Peter Tingle

Scoring:
1–5 correct answers: You've got some movies to watch
6–10 correct answers: You're a mere mortal
11–15 correct answers: You're a superhero!

ULTIMATE ZENDAYA QUIZ

1. *Smallfoot*—Gabriel Gundacker, 2. *Project Runway*, 3. CoverGirl, 4. Kellie Pickler and Derek Hough, 5. Noon, 6. Halley Brandon, 7. Erykah Badu's "Tyrone," 8. Fola, 9. Tweet, 10. *GQ Australia*, 11. The Coleman trudge, 12. Oakland, California, 13. September 1, 1996, 14. Air hockey, 15. Teacher, 16. Michelle "MJ" Jones, 17. "Hot n Cold," 18. *Black-ish*—Rasheida, 19. *Spider-Man: Far from Home*—Michelle (MJ), 20. *Super Buddies*, 21. Sunblock, 22. Prague, 23. Tower Bridge, 24. "Wonderful Life," 25. The theater *(Scoring on next page)*

Scoring:

1–8 correct answers: You need to talk to Darnell

9–16 correct answers: You're respectable

17–21 correct answers: You're pretty dope

22–25 correct answers: You are the Ultimate Zendaya fan!

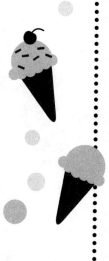

HELP US PICK THE
NEXT ISSUE OF

HERE'S HOW TO VOTE:

Go to

www.ReadScoop.com

to cast your vote for
who we should
SCOOP! next.